Read
Trace
Write
a
un'
l
io
am
am
an
uno
as
come
at
a
AF415741

Read and write the sentence!

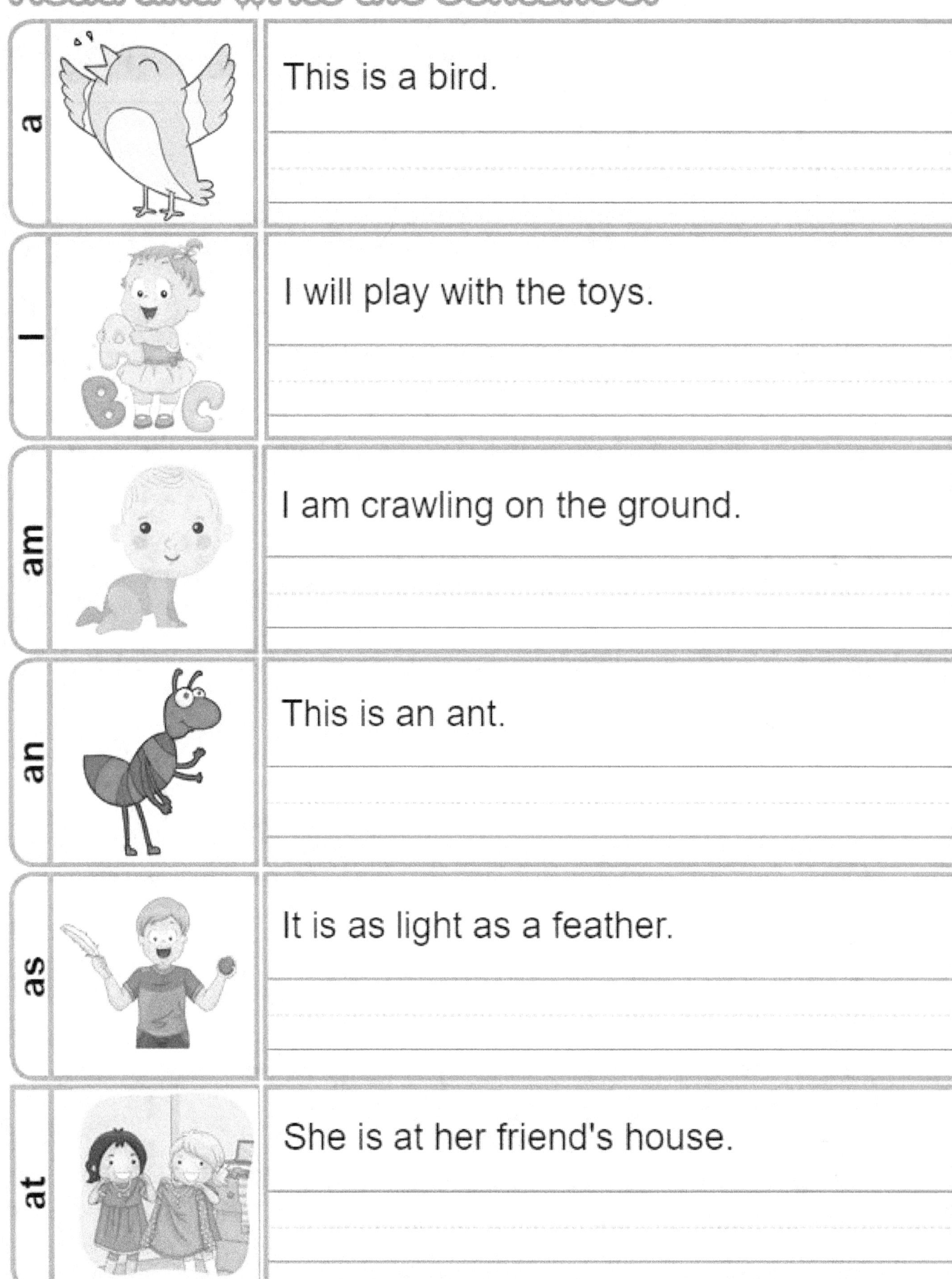

a	This is a bird.
I	I will play with the toys.
am	I am crawling on the ground.
an	This is an ant.
as	It is as light as a feather.
at	She is at her friend's house.

Read
Trace
Write
be
essere
by
di
do
fare
go
partire
he
lui
if
se

Read and write the sentence!

be	We will be friends.
by	This story is by me.
do	She will do the cleaning.
go	He will go somewhere.
he	He is bored.
if	If I put my clothes here, it will get washed.

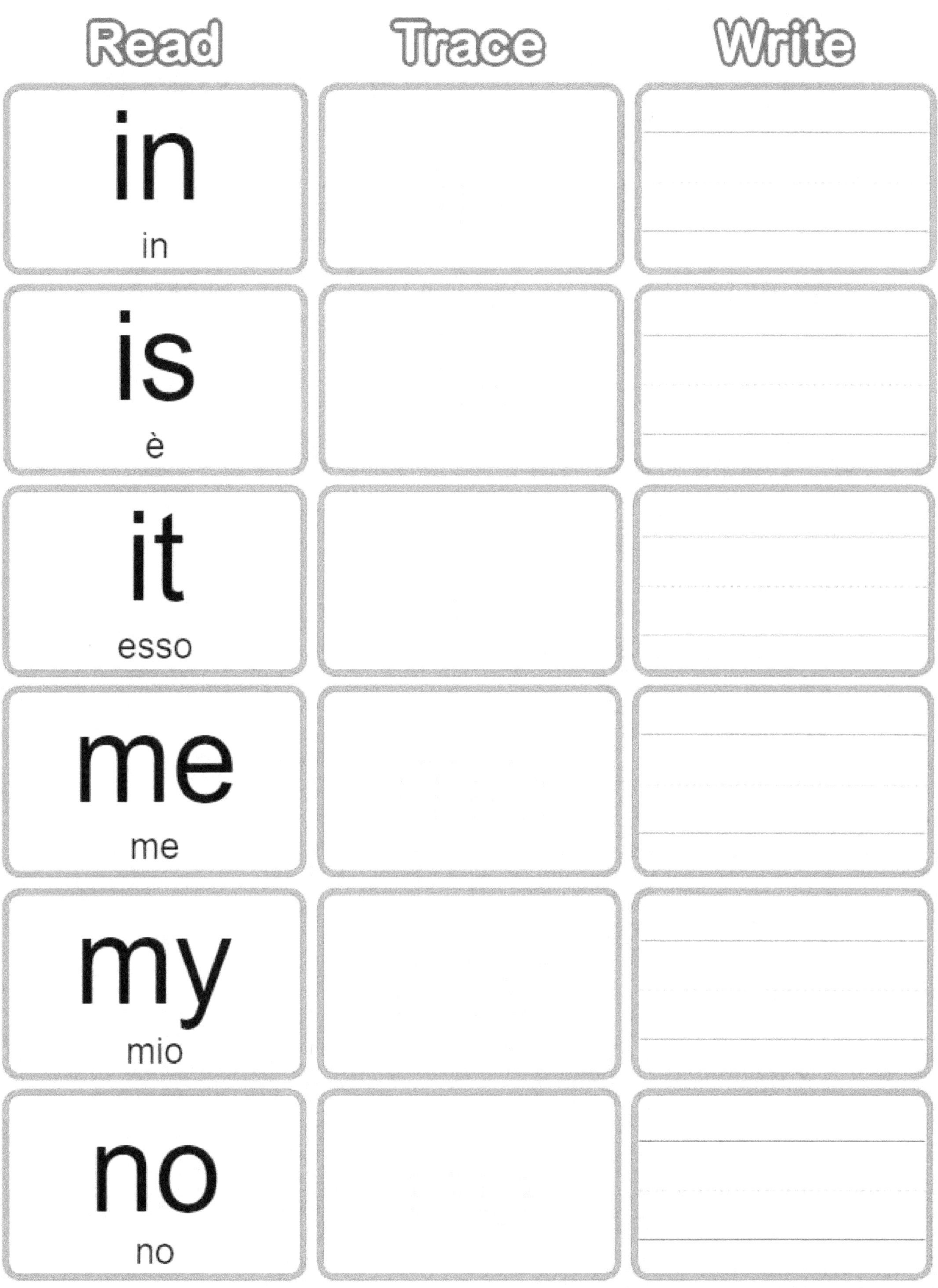

Read
Trace
Write
in
in
is
è
it
esso
me
me
my
mio
no
no

Read and write the sentence!

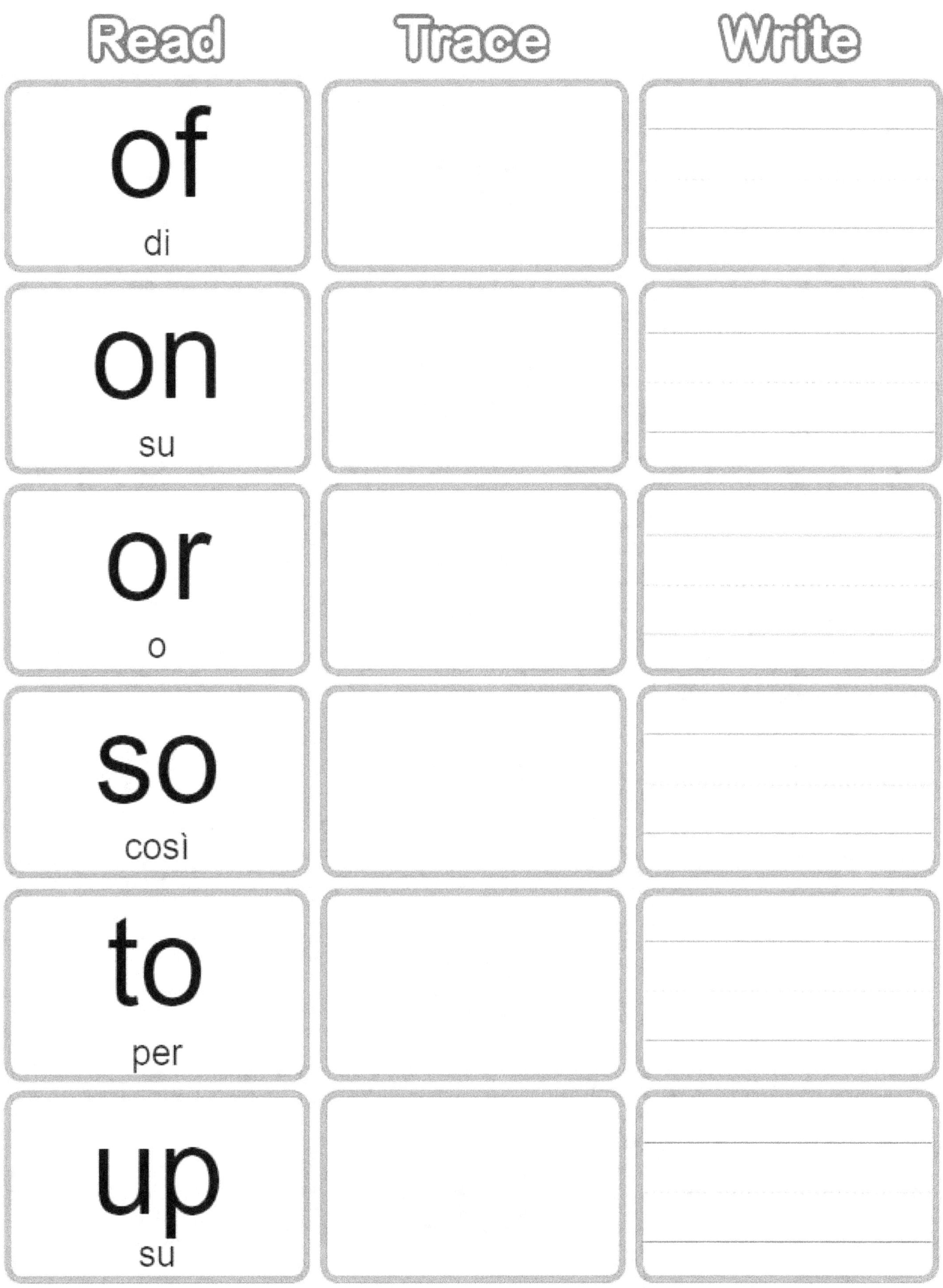
Read
Trace
Write
of
di
on
su
or
o
so
così
to
per
up
su

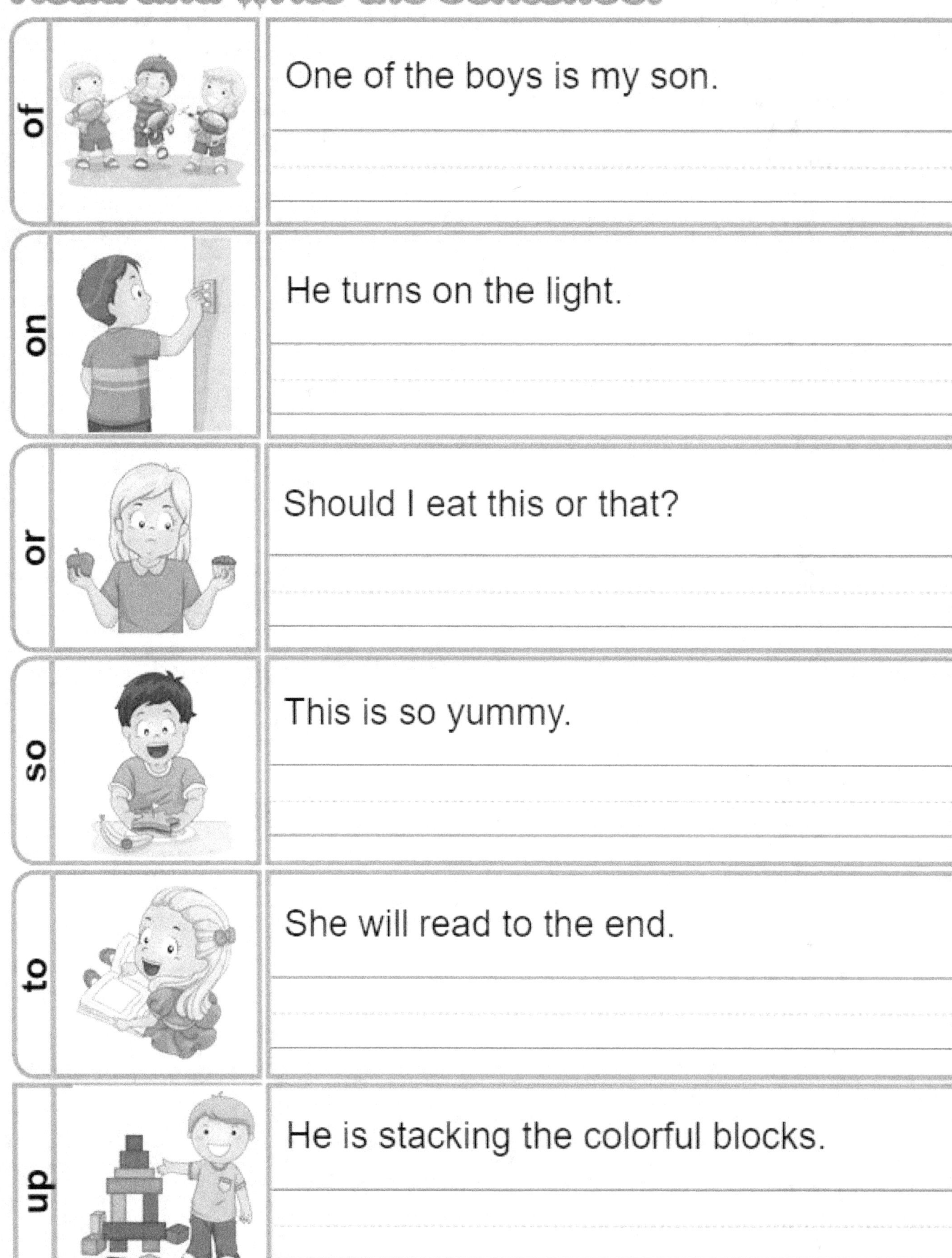

Read and write the sentence!

of

One of the boys is my son.

on

He turns on the light.

or

Should I eat this or that?

so

This is so yummy.

to

She will read to the end.

up

He is stacking the colorful blocks.

Read	Trace	Write
us noi		
we noi		
all tutti		
and e		
any qualunque		
are siamo		

Read and write the sentence!

us	Both of us are walking.
we	We are helping to make a house.
all	We are all dancing together.
and	My brother and I are playing.
any	They can read any books.
are	The eggs are colorful.

Read
Trace
Write
ask
chiedi
ate
mangiò
bed
letto
big
grande
box
scatola
boy
ragazzo

Read and write the sentence!

ask	The girl asks a question.
ate	They ate yummy ice cream.
bed	This bed is for the baby.
big	The bottle is very big.
box	The box has all my toys.
boy	The boy is hiding behind it.

Read
Trace
Write
but
ma
buy
acquistare
can
può
car
auto
cat
gatto
cow
mucca

Read and write the sentence!

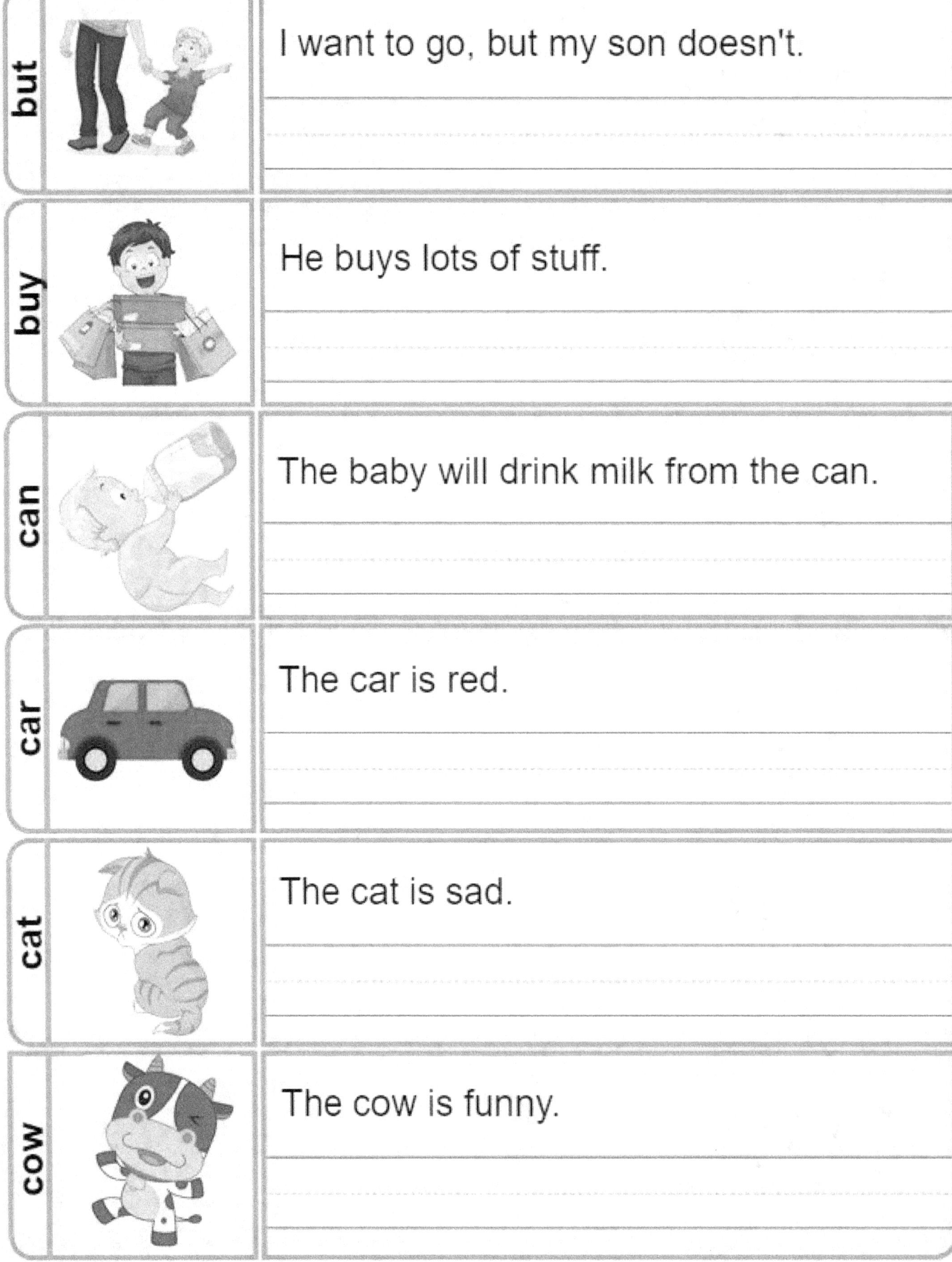

but	I want to go, but my son doesn't.
buy	He buys lots of stuff.
can	The baby will drink milk from the can.
car	The car is red.
cat	The cat is sad.
cow	The cow is funny.

Read
Trace
Write
cut
taglio
day
giorno
did
fatto
dog
cane
eat
mangiare
egg
uovo

Read and write the sentence!

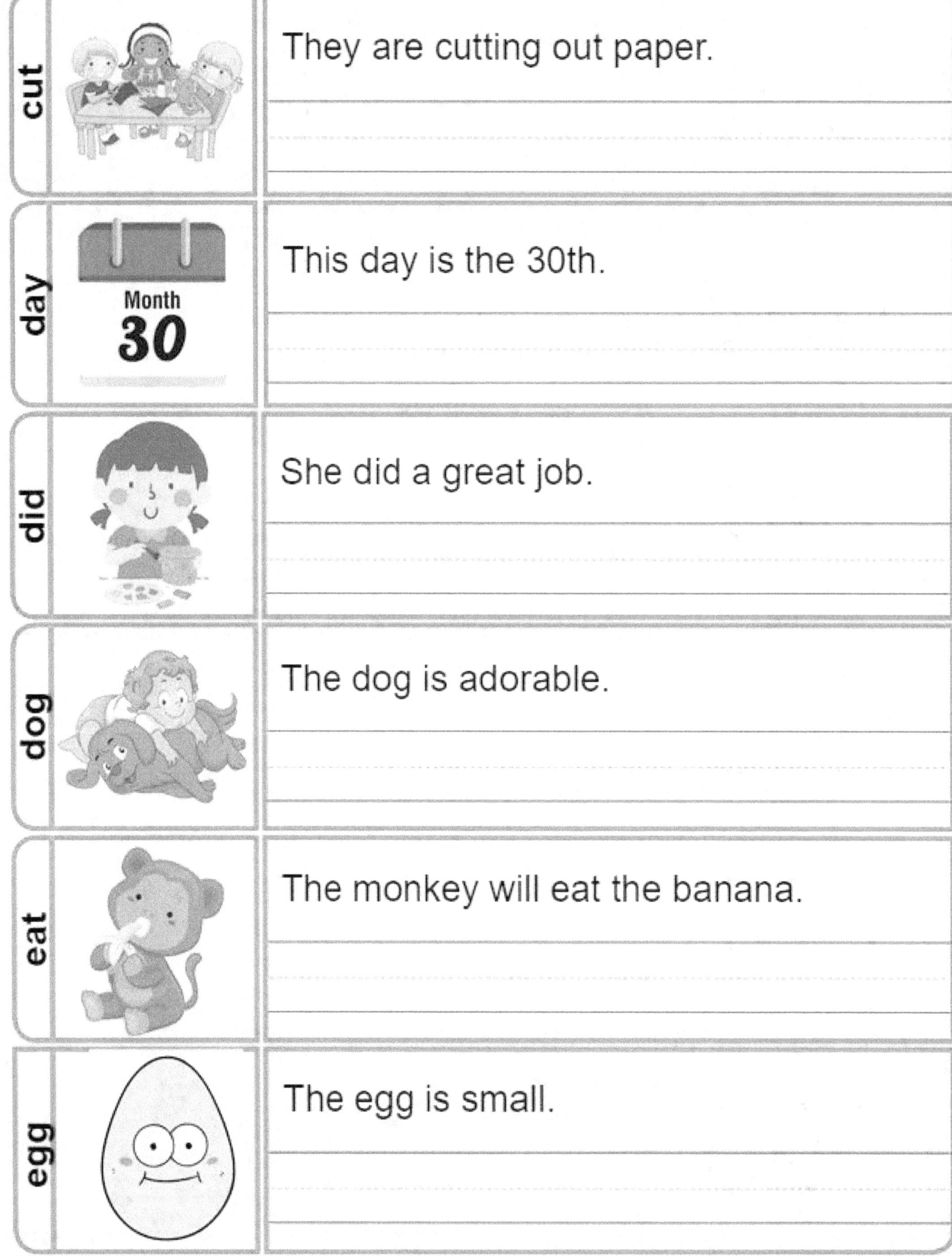

Read
Trace
Write
eye
occhio
far
lontano
fly
volare
for
per
get
ottenere
got
avuto

Read and write the sentence!

eye — The fox is closing his eyes.

far — He can fly the plane very far.

fly — The bee will fly back home.

for — The dog is begging for food.

get — He will get a trophy.

got — The baby got some new toys.

Read	Trace	Write
had aveva		
has ha		
her sua		
him lui		
his il suo		
hot caldo		

Read and write the sentence!

had		He had a big tummy.
has		She has a doll.
her		She has her trolley.
him		I gave my hat to him.
his		His cheeks are big.
hot		It is hot on the beach.

Read
Trace
Write
how
come
its
suo
leg
gamba
let
permettere
man
uomo
may
maggio

Read and write the sentence!

how	How many blocks are there?
its	Its legs are short.
leg	His legs are short.
let	Let me come in!
man	The man is a vet.
may	May I have more?

Read	Trace	Write
men uomini		
new nuovo		
not non		
now adesso		
off via		
old vecchio		

Read and write the sentence!

men		The men are mining for gold.
new		She has a new hat.
not		She is not feeling well.
now		Now I am doing my homework.
off		They cut off the paper.
old		You are one year old!

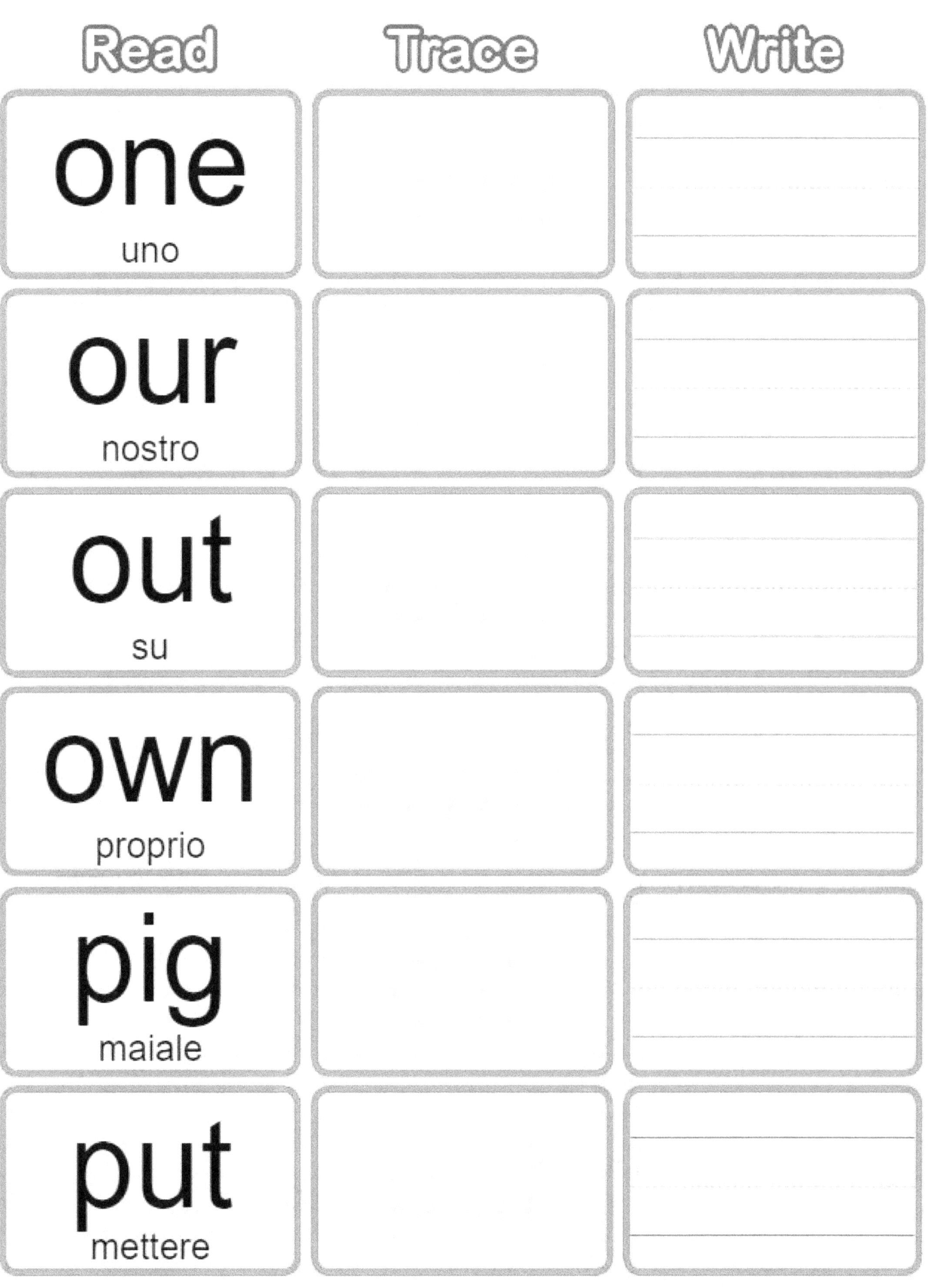

Read
Trace
Write
one
uno
our
nostro
out
su
own
proprio
pig
maiale
put
mettere

Read and write the sentence!

one		The panda says one.
our		This is our room.
out		He will go out.
own		The man owns a computer.
pig		She is sleeping on her pig.
put		She is putting an arm around her daughter.

Read and write the sentence!

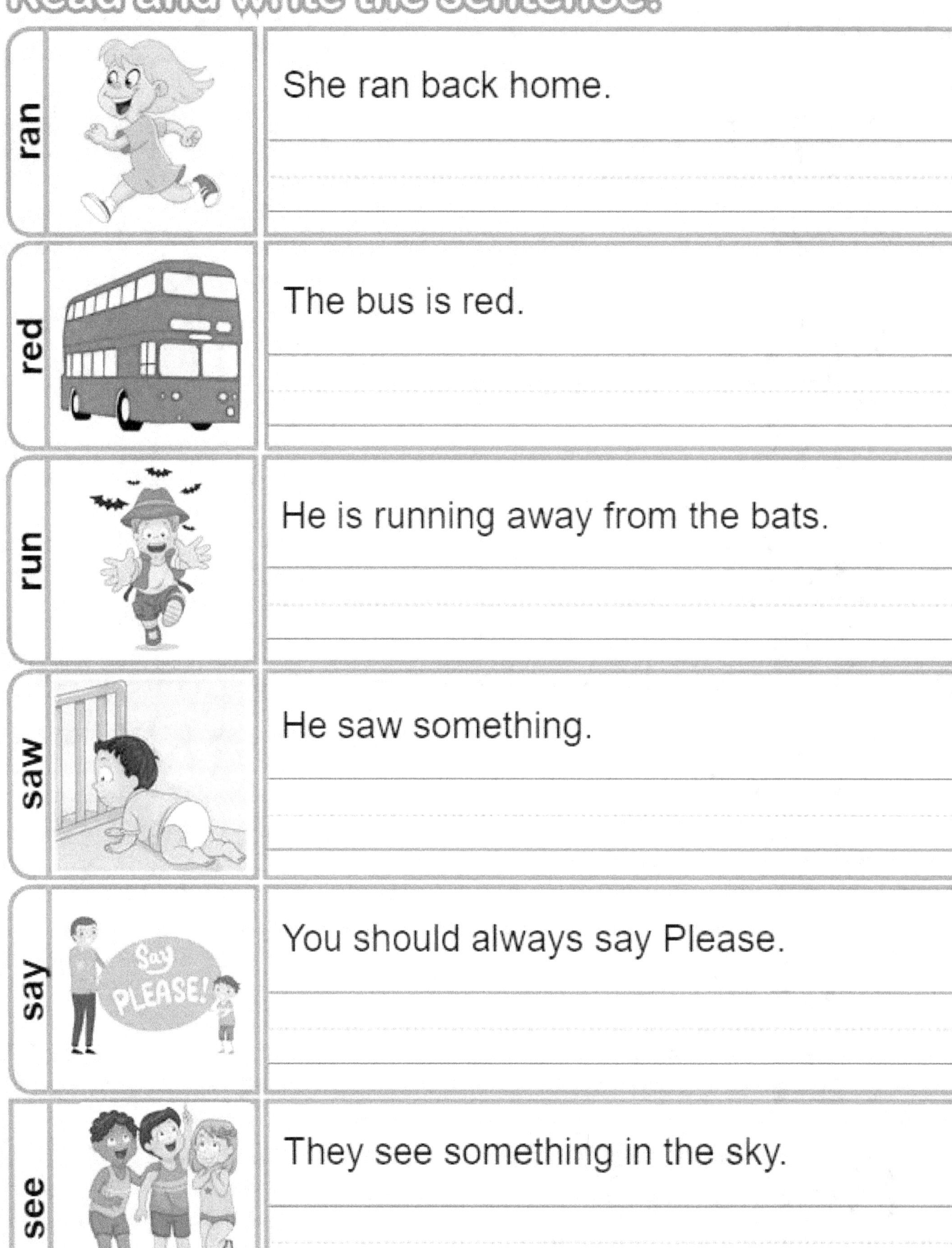

ran		She ran back home.
red		The bus is red.
run		He is running away from the bats.
saw		He saw something.
say		You should always say Please.
see		They see something in the sky.

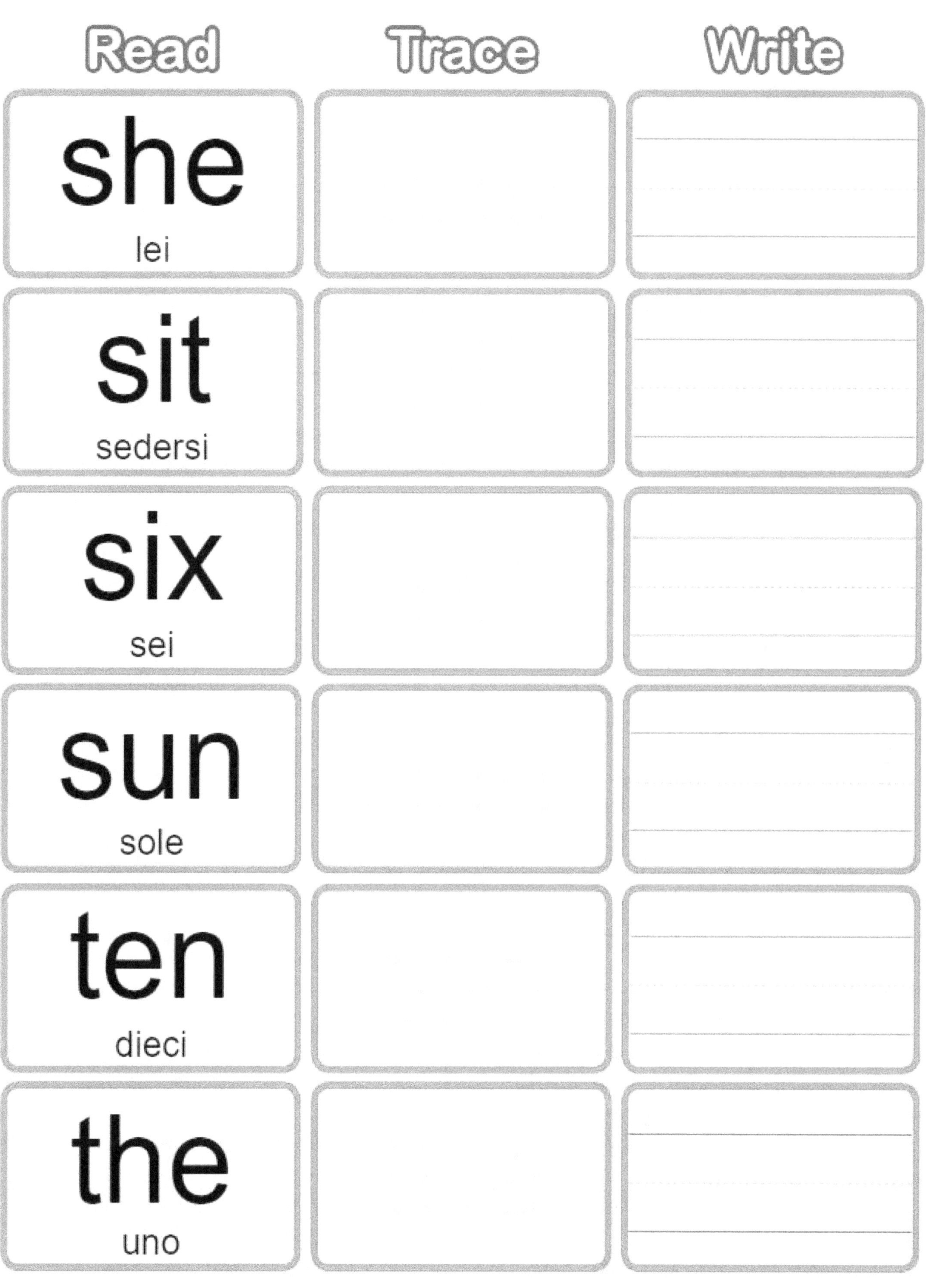
Read
Trace
Write
she
lei
sit
sedersi
six
sei
sun
sole
ten
dieci
the
uno

Read and write the sentence!

Read
Trace
Write
too
pure
top
superiore
toy
giocattolo
try
provare
two
due
use
uso

Read and write the sentence!

too		The bear is too cute.
top		The pot is on the top.
toy		The baby has lots of toys.
try		We try to be kind to him.
two		Today you have turned two.
use		I use my toothpaste and toothbrush.

<table>
<tr><th>Read</th><th>Trace</th><th>Write</th></tr>
<tr><td>was
era</td><td></td><td></td></tr>
<tr><td>way
modo</td><td></td><td></td></tr>
<tr><td>who
che cosa</td><td></td><td></td></tr>
<tr><td>why
perché</td><td></td><td></td></tr>
<tr><td>yes
sì</td><td></td><td></td></tr>
<tr><td>you
voi</td><td></td><td></td></tr>
</table>

Read and write the sentence!

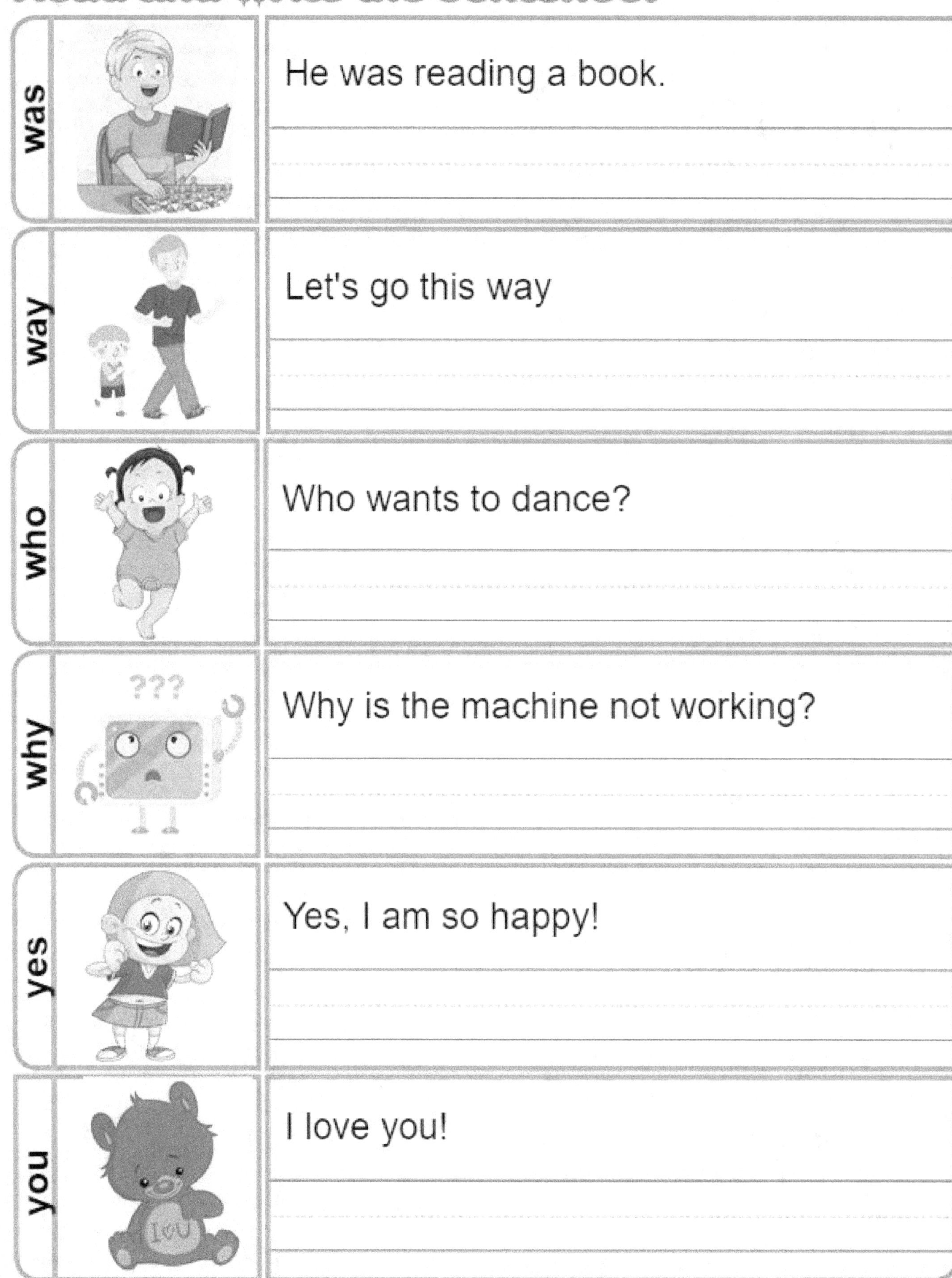

was	He was reading a book.
way	Let's go this way
who	Who wants to dance?
why	Why is the machine not working?
yes	Yes, I am so happy!
you	I love you!

Read
Trace
Write

away
lontano

baby
bambino

back
indietro

ball
palla

bear
orso

been
era

Read and write the sentence!

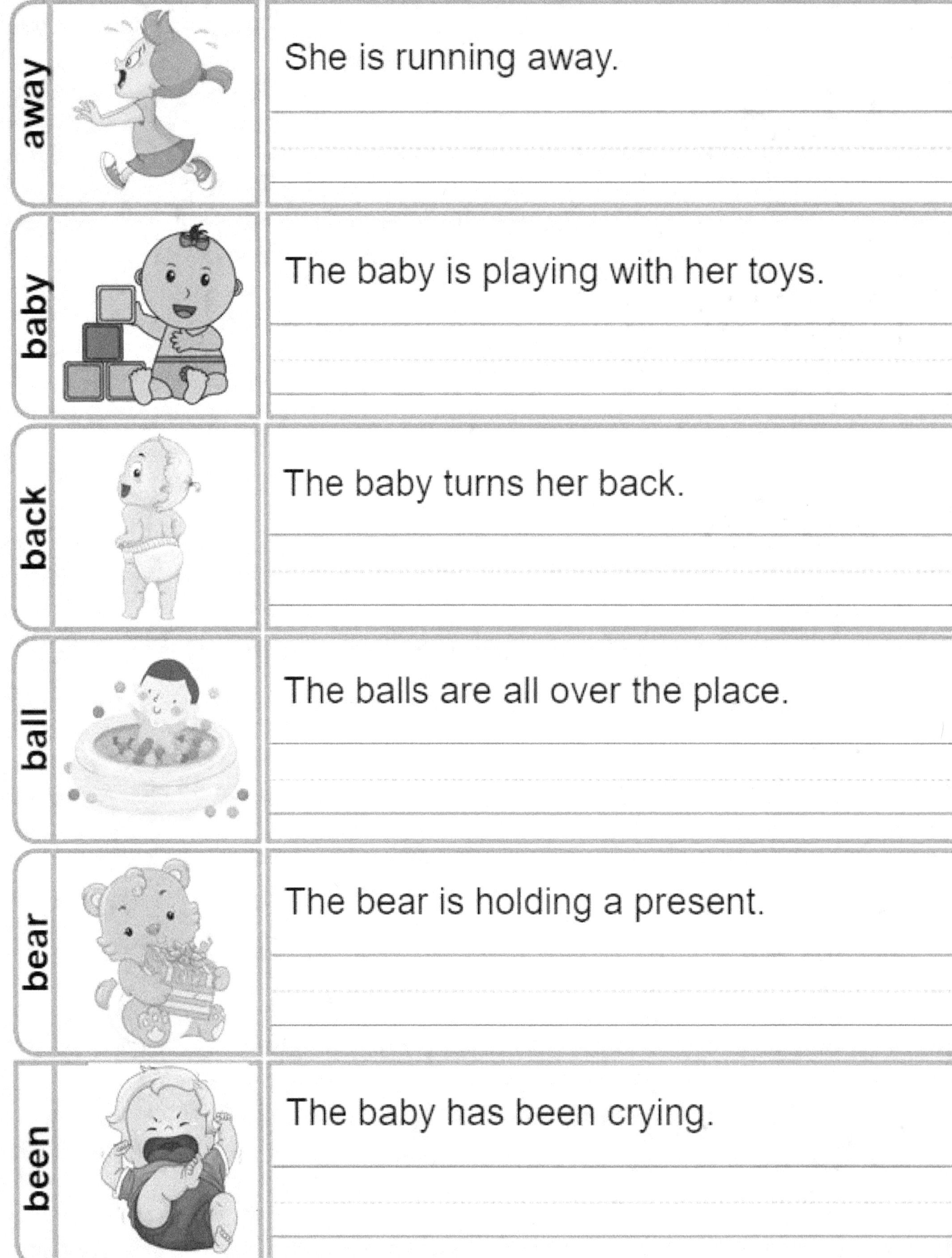

away	She is running away.
baby	The baby is playing with her toys.
back	The baby turns her back.
ball	The balls are all over the place.
bear	The bear is holding a present.
been	The baby has been crying.

Read	Trace	Write
bell campana		
best migliore		
bird uccello		
blue blu		
boat barca		
both tutti e due		

Read and write the sentence!

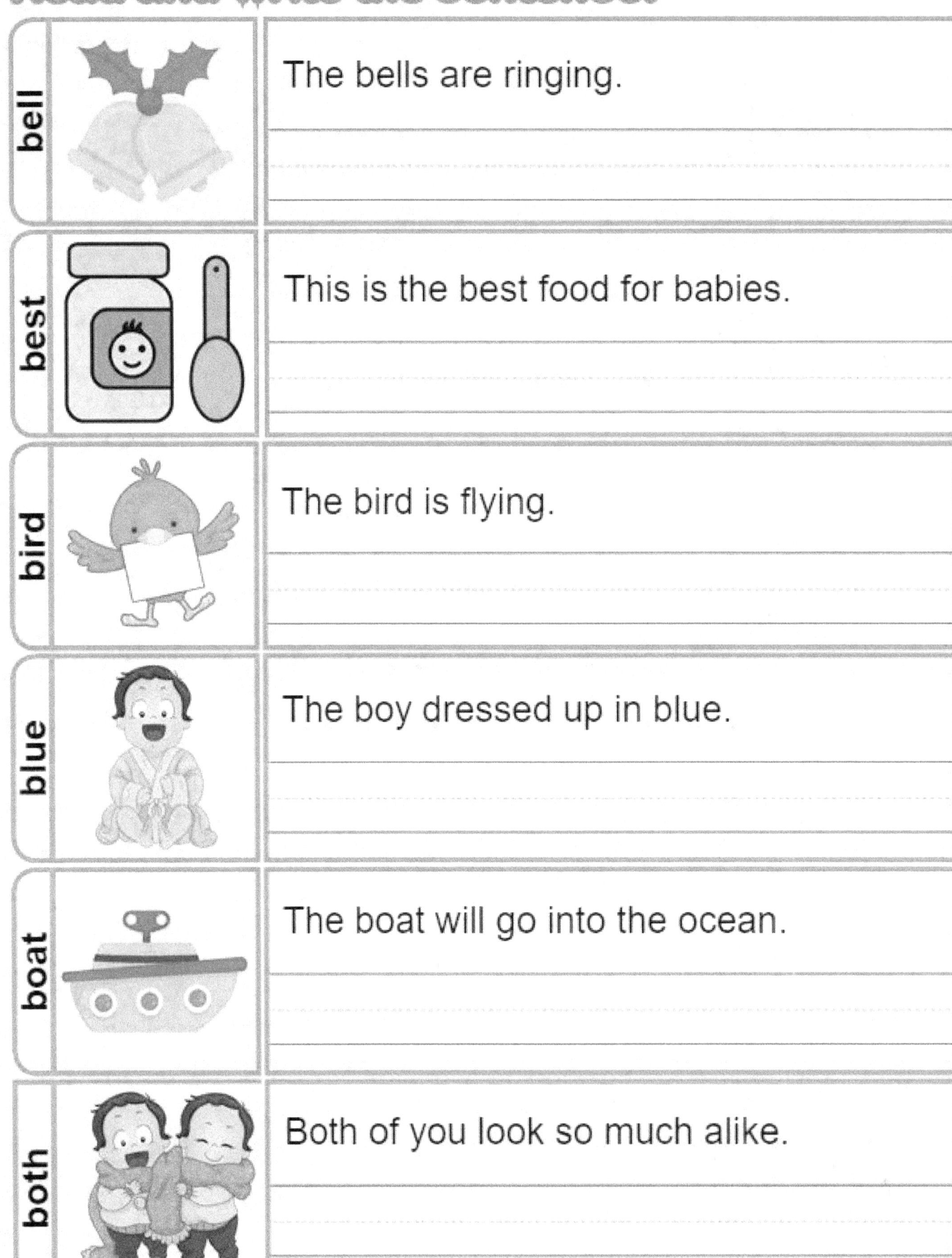

Read	Trace	Write
cake torta		
call chiamata		
came è venuto		
coat cappotto		
cold freddo		
come venire		

Read and write the sentence!

Read
Trace
Write
corn
mais
does
fa
doll
bambola
done
fatto
door
porta
down
giù

Read and write the sentence!

corn	The corn tastes good.
does	Does that thing taste bad?
doll	She is hugging her doll.
done	I've done reading my book.
door	They open the door.
down	The boy turns his head down.

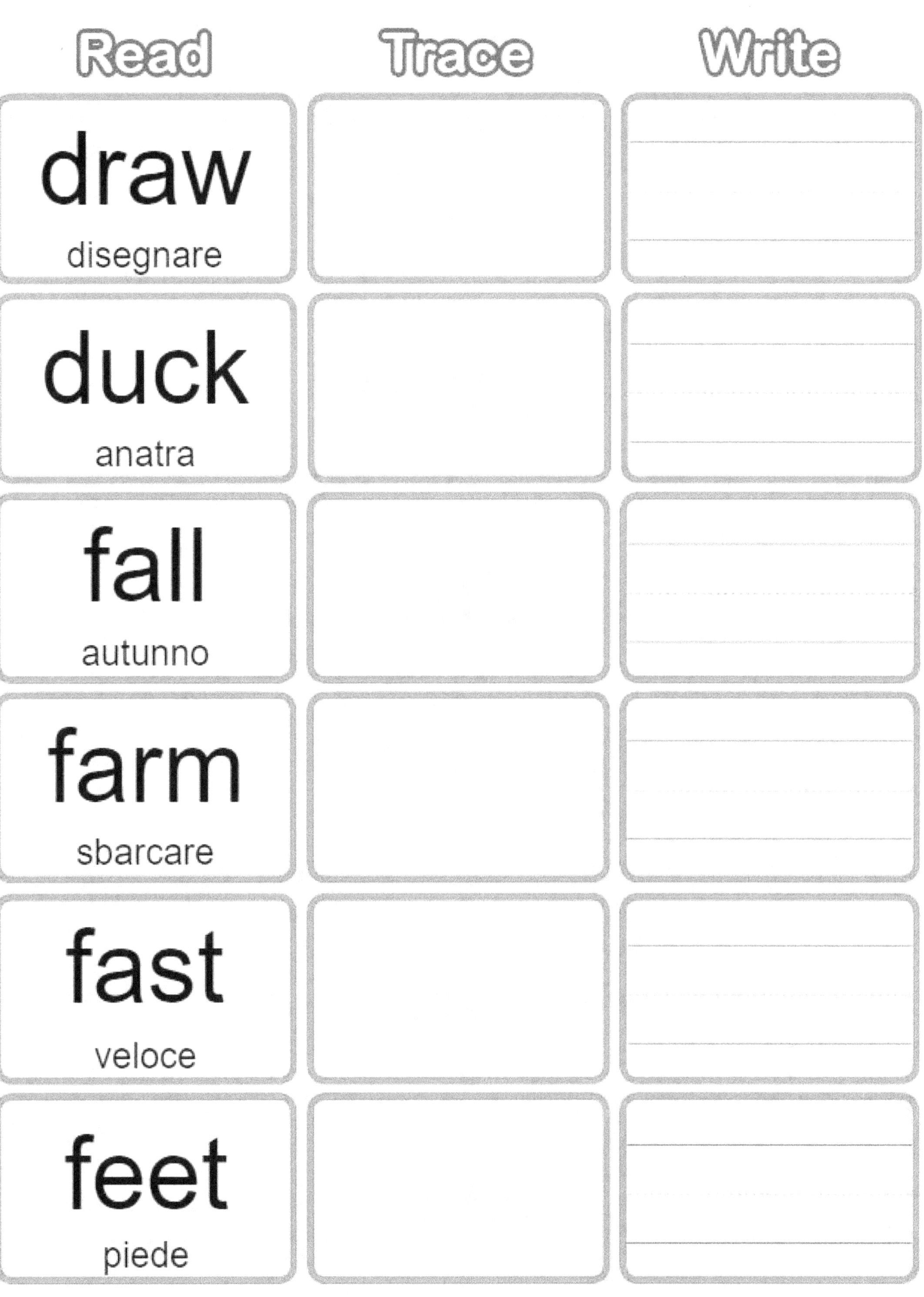

Read
Trace
Write
draw
disegnare
duck
anatra
fall
autunno
farm
sbarcare
fast
veloce
feet
piede

Read and write the sentence!

draw	They all draw pictures.
duck	The duck is yellow.
fall	He fell down from the swing.
farm	He grows crops at his farm.
fast	She is doing everything very fast.
feet	I touch my feet.

Read	Trace	Write
find trova		
fire fuoco		
fish pesce		
five cinque		
four quattro		
from a partire dal		

Read and write the sentence!

find		They are finding something.
fire		The fire is blazing and dangerous.
fish		The fish are swimming in the ocean.
five		You get birthday gifts for turning five.
four		The lion is turning four today.
from		She will draw a picture of her flower.

Read
Trace
Write
full
pieno
game
giochi
gave
ha dato
girl
ragazza
give
dare
goes
va

Read and write the sentence!

Read	Trace	Write
good bene		
grow crescere		
hand mano		
have avere		
head testa		
help aiuto		

Read and write the sentence!

good	The baby is acting very well today.
grow	My plant will grow!
hand	My hand is touching the wall.
have	She will have lots of friends.
head	My head is round.
help	They help each other wash the clothes.

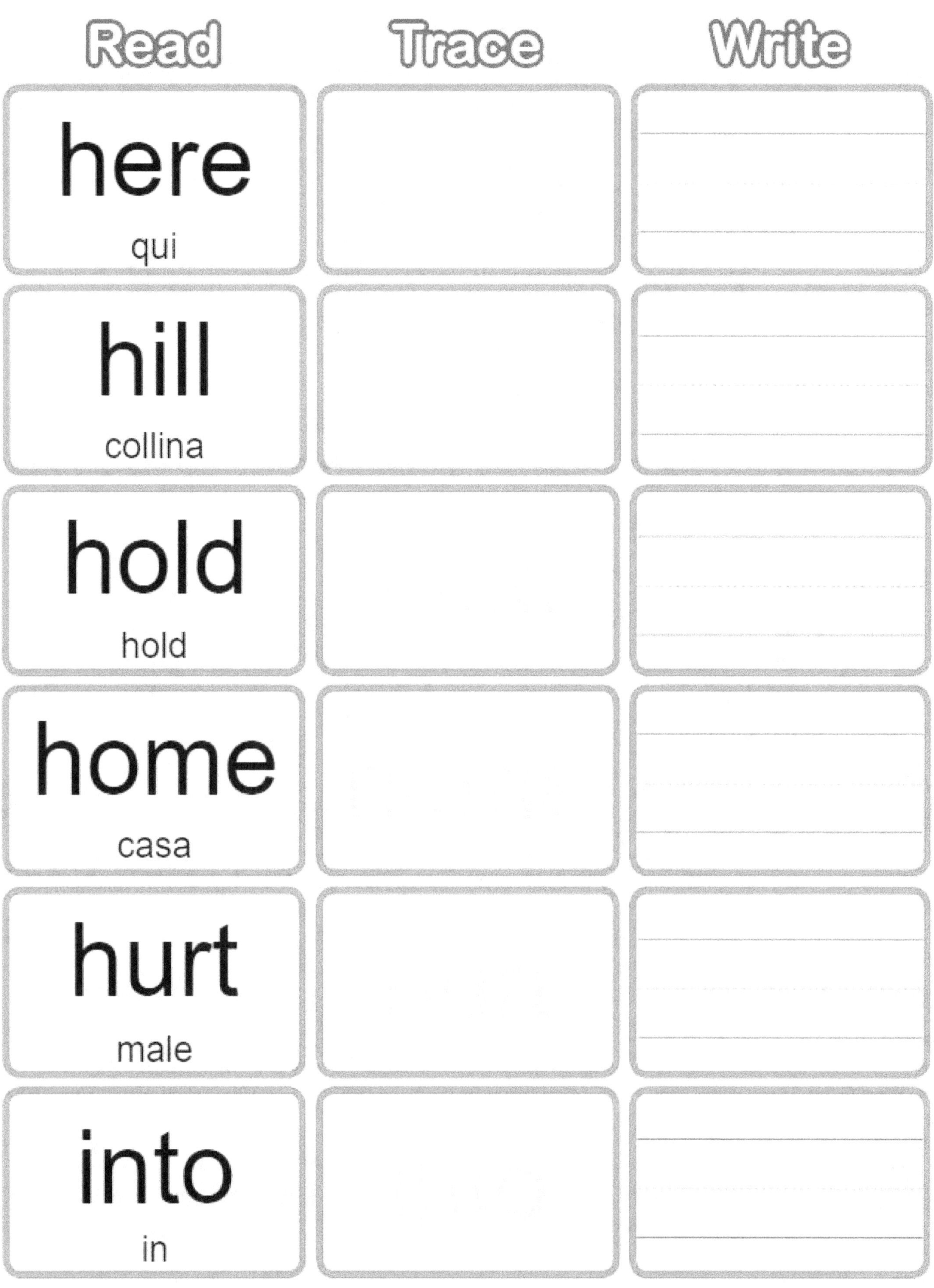

Read
Trace
Write
here
qui
hill
collina
hold
hold
home
casa
hurt
male
into
in

Read and write the sentence!

here	America is over here.
hill	The hill has some trees and a house.
hold	He is holding his daughter.
home	He drew a picture of his home.
hurt	The boy is hurt.
into	He will jump into the pool.

Read	Trace	Write
jump saltare		
just appena		
keep mantenere		
kind genere		
know conoscere		
like piace		

Read and write the sentence!

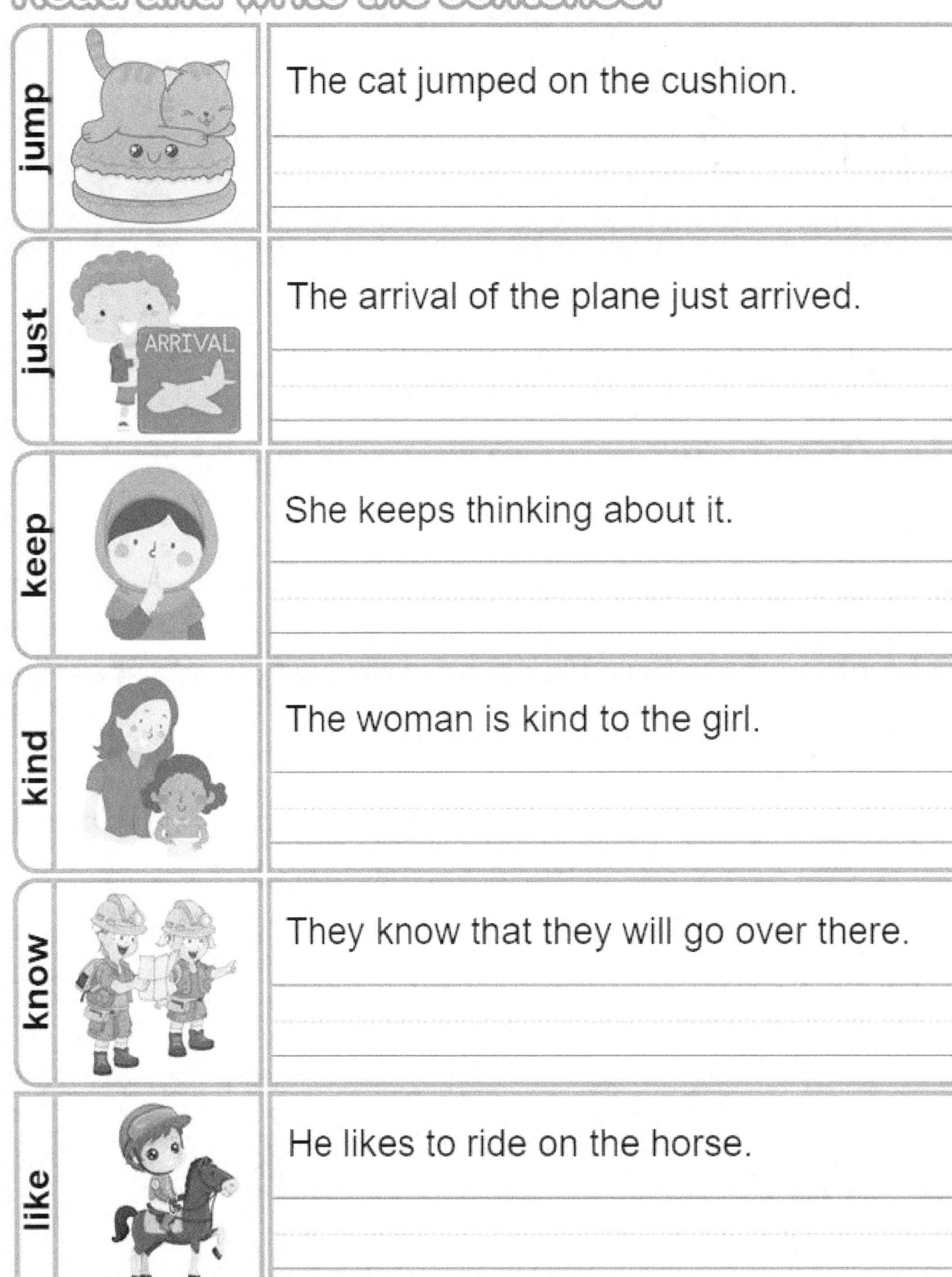

jump	The cat jumped on the cushion.
just	The arrival of the plane just arrived.
keep	She keeps thinking about it.
kind	The woman is kind to the girl.
know	They know that they will go over there.
like	He likes to ride on the horse.

Read
Trace
Write
live
vivere
long
lungo
look
guarda
made
fatto
make
fatto
many
molti

Read and write the sentence!

live — They all live together.

long — The pencil is very long.

look — They are looking at something.

made — They made a promise.

make — They are going to make something.

many — He has many shirts.

Read	Trace	Write
milk latte		
much tanto		
must dovere		
name nome		
nest nido		
once una volta		

Read and write the sentence!

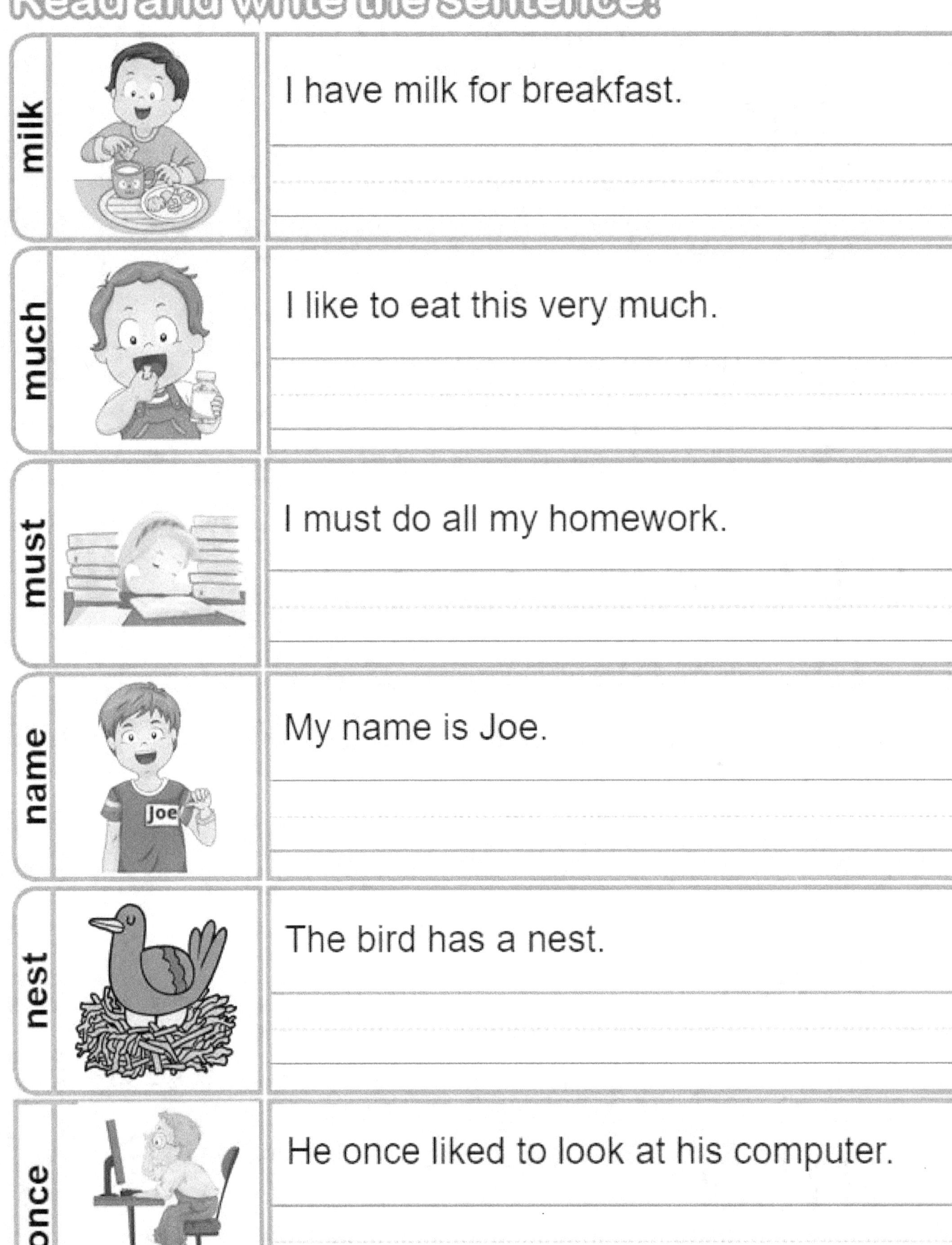

Read	Trace	Write
only solo		
open aperto		
over al di sopra di		
pick raccogliere		
play giocare		
pull tirare		

Read and write the sentence!

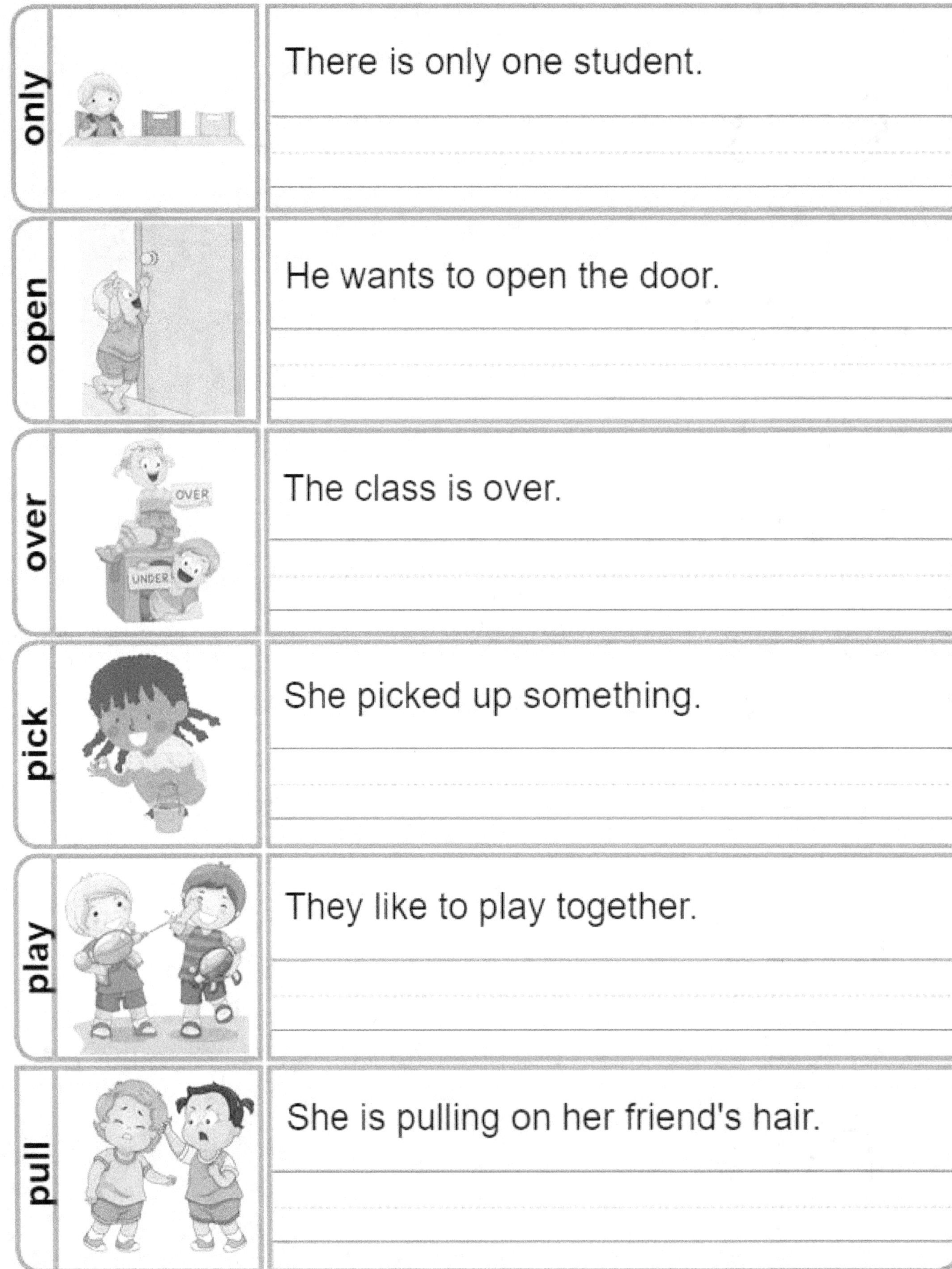

only	There is only one student.
open	He wants to open the door.
over	The class is over.
pick	She picked up something.
play	They like to play together.
pull	She is pulling on her friend's hair.

Read
Trace
Write

rain
pioggia

read
leggere

ride
giro

ring
squillare

said
disse

seed
seme

Read and write the sentence!

rain	The rain is not going to hit us.
read	She likes to read books.
ride	The baby is riding on a toy horse.
ring	The bird is holding a ring in its beak.
said	She said hello to her neighbor.
seed	The seeds are going to plant.

Read
Trace
Write
shoe
scarpa
show
mostrare
sing
cantare
snow
neve
some
alcuni
song
canzone

shoe	Her shoes are cute and purple.
show	This map shows the location.
sing	The baby can sing along.
snow	I like to play snow.
some	These are some of my toys.
song	I will sing a song in the talent show.

Read
Trace
Write
soon
presto
stop
fermare
take
prendere
tell
raccontare
that
quello
them
loro

Read and write the sentence!

soon	The eggs will hatch soon.
stop	The teacher says to stop.
take	They take some flowers.
tell	She is telling a story.
that	That bird dressed up as Santa.
them	He likes to eat them.

Read	Trace	Write

then
poi

they
essi

this
questo

time
tempo

tree
albero

upon
su

Read and write the sentence!

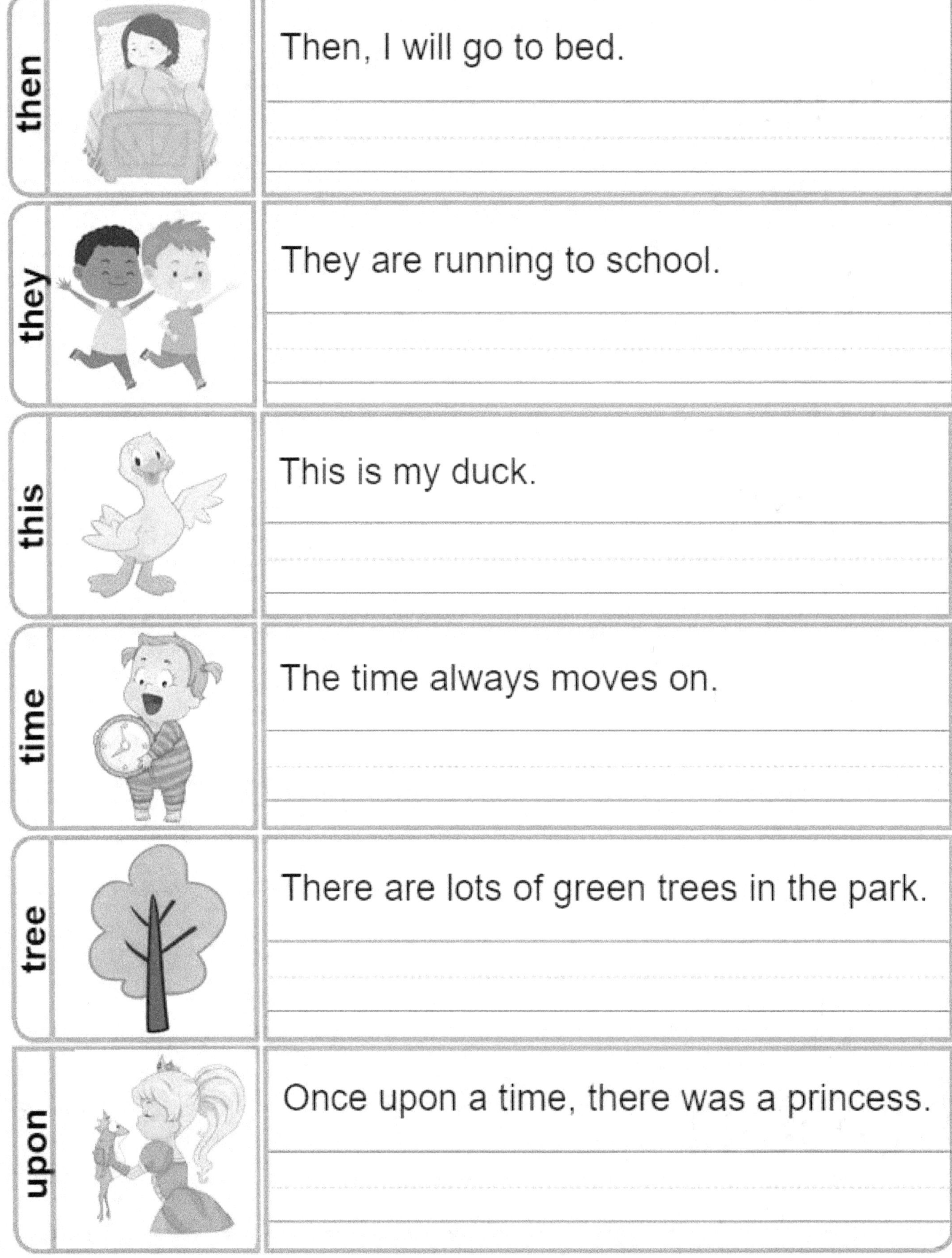

then	Then, I will go to bed.
they	They are running to school.
this	This is my duck.
time	The time always moves on.
tree	There are lots of green trees in the park.
upon	Once upon a time, there was a princess.

Read	Trace	Write
very molto		
walk camminare		
want volere		
warm caldo		
wash lavaggio		
well bene		

Read and write the sentence!

very		The baby is lovely.
walk		They are walking on the sidewalk.
want		The baby wants more milk.
warm		The bath is warm.
wash		She is going to wash the dishes.
well		He can save money well.

Read	Trace	Write

went
andato

were
siamo

what
che cosa

when
quando

will
volere

wind
vento

Read and write the sentence!

went	 The crocodile went to the pond.
were	 There were lots of toys.
what	 What is the lion doing?
when	 When are you going to wake up?
will	 Will I get it in?
wind	 The wind is blowing fiercely.

Read	Trace	Write
wish desiderio		
with con		
wood legna		
work lavoro		
your il tuo		
about di		

Read and write the sentence!

wish	I wish you a happy Christmas!
with	He is with his sister.
wood	He is stacking up wooden blocks.
work	He is going to work in his tractor.
your	Your baby is wearing a yellow suit.
about	It's about to be 12:30.

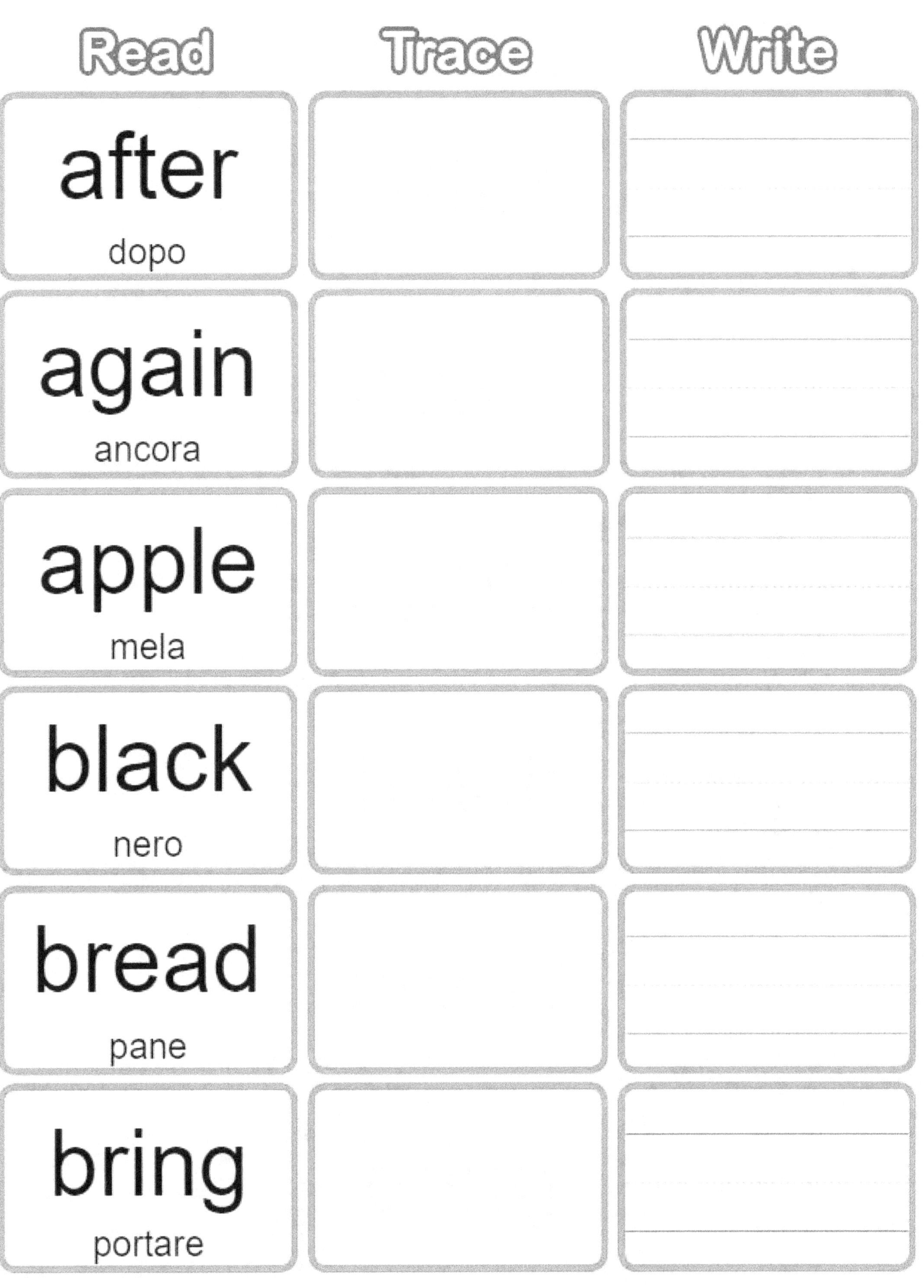

Read
Trace
Write
after
dopo
again
ancora
apple
mela
black
nero
bread
pane
bring
portare

after	The teacher calmed them after they fought.
again	He did it again!
apple	The apple is red and juicy.
black	The crow is black.
bread	My breakfast is bread and jam.
bring	He is bringing his project.

Read	Trace	Write
brown marrone		
carry trasportare		
chair sedia		
clean pulito		
could poteva		
don't non fare		

Read and write the sentence!

brown	Her stuffed animal is a brown bear.
carry	He is carrying a big crayon.
chair	He is sitting on his chair.
clean	He needs to clean up.
could	The baby could do push-ups.
don't	Don't do that!

Read	Trace	Write
drink bevanda		
eight otto		
every ogni		
first primo		
floor pavimento		
found trovato		

Read and write the sentence!

	The baby likes to drink water.
drink	

	You get eight gifts for turning eight!
eight	

	Every book is colorful.
every	

	We won first place.
first	

	She is sitting on the floor.
floor	

	It found a hat in the streets.
found	

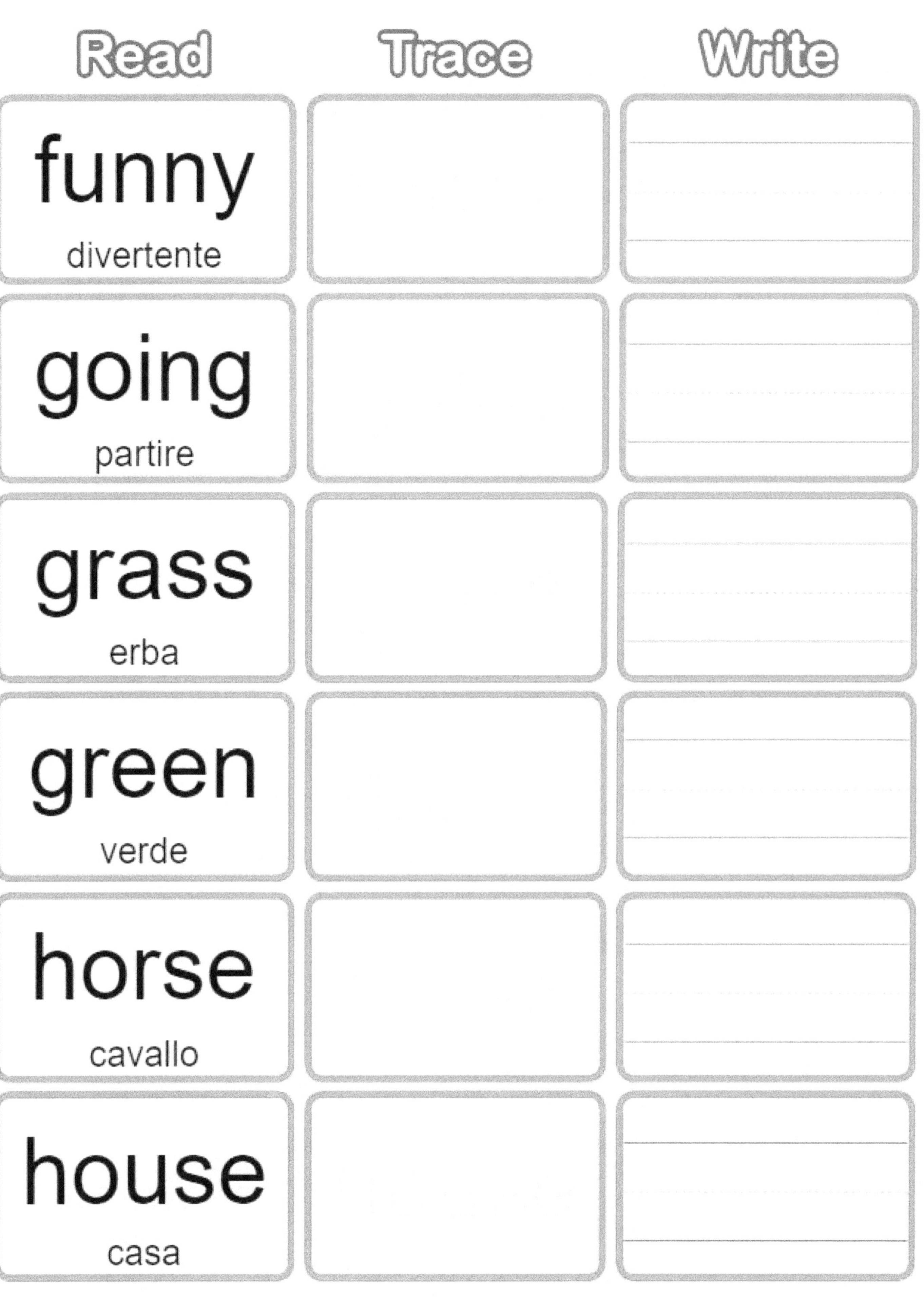

Read
Trace
Write
funny
divertente
going
partire
grass
erba
green
verde
horse
cavallo
house
casa

Read and write the sentence!

funny	The rabbit thinks the joke is funny.
going	The bear is going to eat all the honey.
grass	The goat eats grass on the hill.
green	The turtle that is walking is green.
horse	The horse is magical.
house	They lived in that house.

Read	Trace	Write
kitty gatto		
laugh ridere		
light leggero		
money i soldi		
never mai		
night notte		

Read and write the sentence!

kitty	The kitties are charming.
laugh	They are laughing while playing.
light	The boy will turn on the lights.
money	I have earned a lot of money.
never	The bear never ate ice cream before.
night	I will sleep on my blanket at night.

Read	Trace	Write
paper carta		
party festa		
right corretta		
round il giro		
seven sette		
shall deve		

Read and write the sentence!

paper	I will draw on the paper for a project.
party	The party will be for her birthday.
right	They say we have to go right.
round	The frogs' eyes are round.
seven	The monkey can count to seven.
shall	Shall I make a garden?

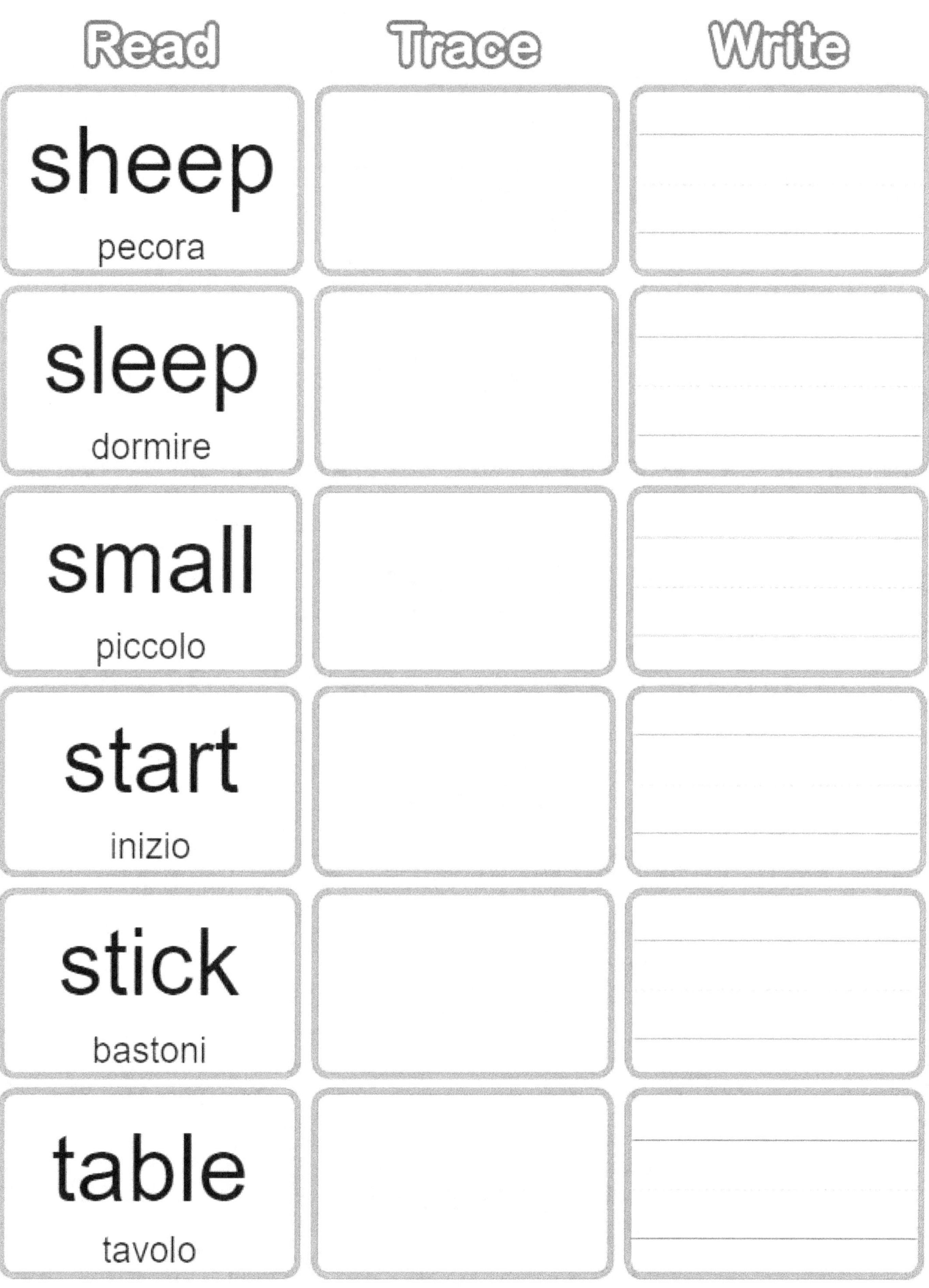

Read
Trace
Write
sheep
pecora
sleep
dormire
small
piccolo
start
inizio
stick
bastoni
table
tavolo

Read and write the sentence!

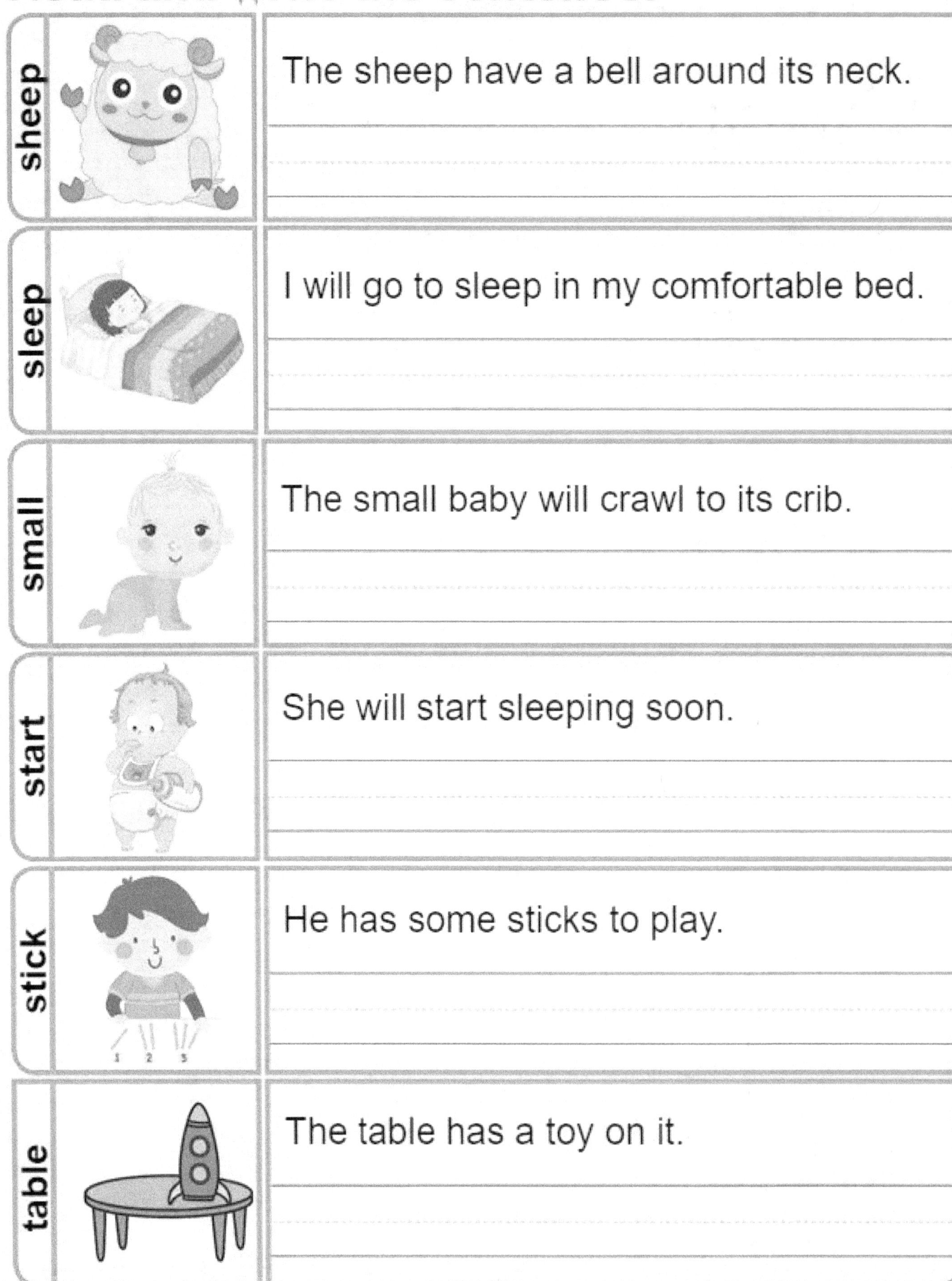

sheep	The sheep have a bell around its neck.
sleep	I will go to sleep in my comfortable bed.
small	The small baby will crawl to its crib.
start	She will start sleeping soon.
stick	He has some sticks to play.
table	The table has a toy on it.

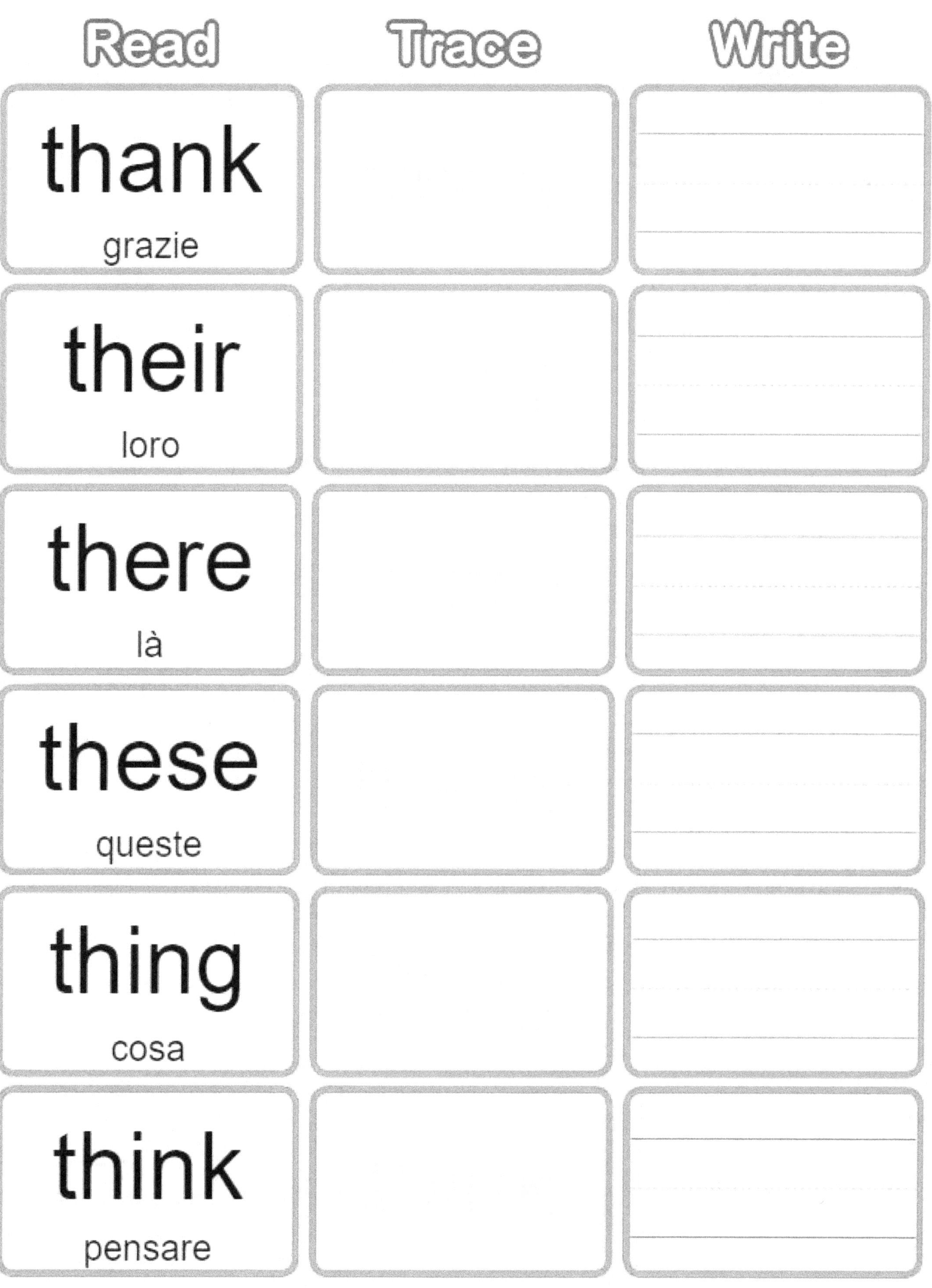# Read   Trace   Write

Read	Trace	Write
thank grazie		
their loro		
there là		
these queste		
thing cosa		
think pensare		

Read and write the sentence!

thank	He made a Thank you card for you.
their	They will enjoy their picnic.
there	There is something in front of you.
these	These are my eating material.
thing	The thing is broken.
think	She thinks about what she is going to draw.

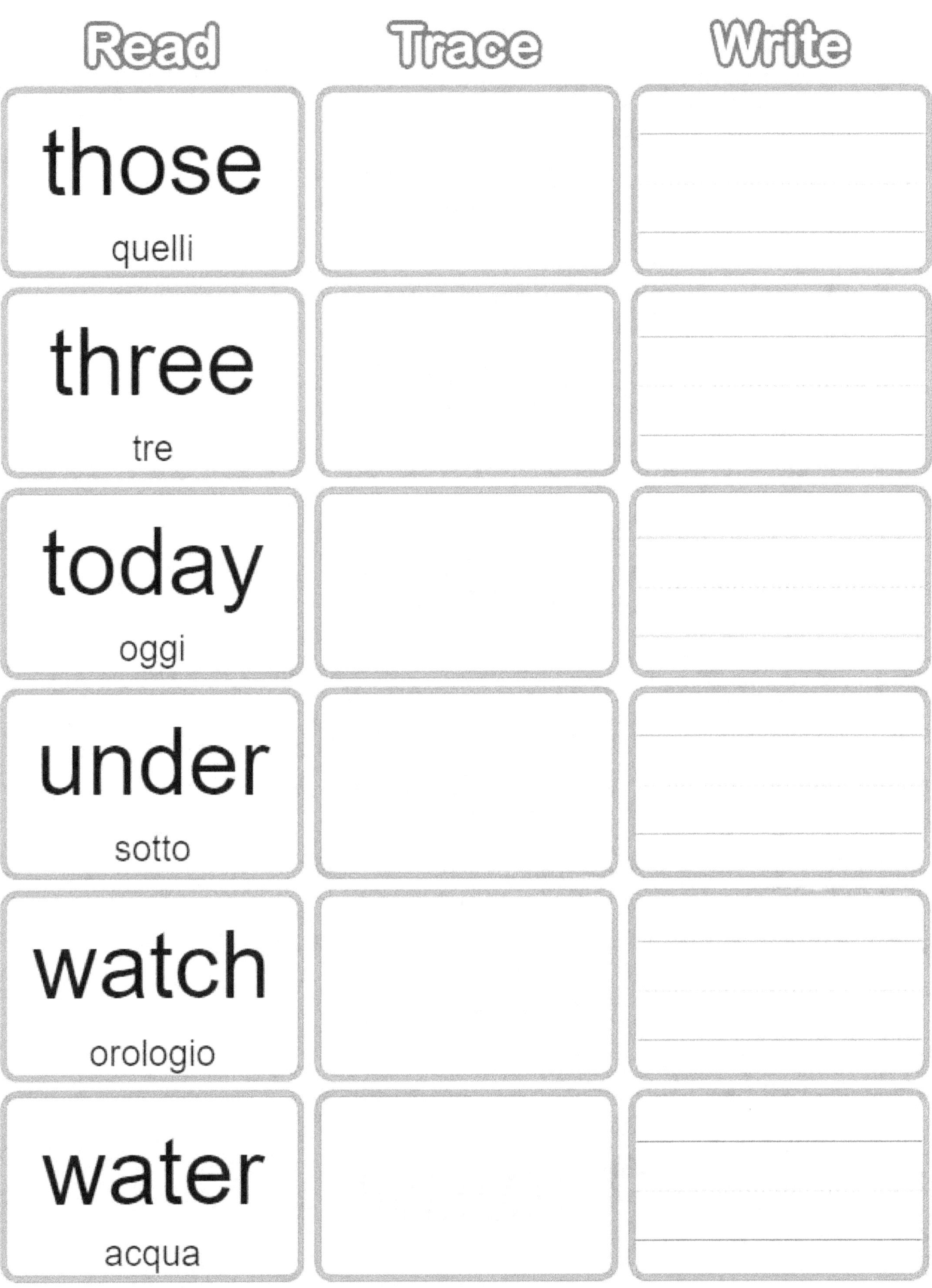

Read	Trace	Write
those quelli		
three tre		
today oggi		
under sotto		
watch orologio		
water acqua		

Read and write the sentence!

those		Those are mine.
three		She will turn three today.
today		Today is a beautiful day.
under		The puppy sleeps under the blanket.
watch		They both watch the video.
water		He is drinking water after a long soccer game.

Read
Trace
Write
where
dove
which
quale
white
bianca
would
voluto
write
scrivi
always
sempre

Read and write the sentence!

where	Where are we?
which	The clothes which are my sisters are colorful.
white	The sheep have white wool.
would	He would tell them a story.
write	I like to write lots of stories.
always	I am always happy that it is Christmas.

Read	Trace	Write
around in giro		
before prima		
better meglio		
farmer contadino		
father padre		
flower fiore		

Read and write the sentence!

around		I will shuffle the shapes around.
before		Before I go to school, I kiss my mom.
better		I can make it better.
farmer		The farmer takes care of the animals.
father		My father is wearing a blue shirt.
flower		She will play with the flowers.

Read	Trace	Write
garden giardino		
ground terra		
letter lettere		
little poco		
mother madre		
myself me stessa		

garden
Her garden is vast and healthy.

ground
I am playing with my dog on the ground.

letter
These are the letters A, B, and C.

little
The world is small.

mother
My mother is very nice.

myself
I made these by myself.

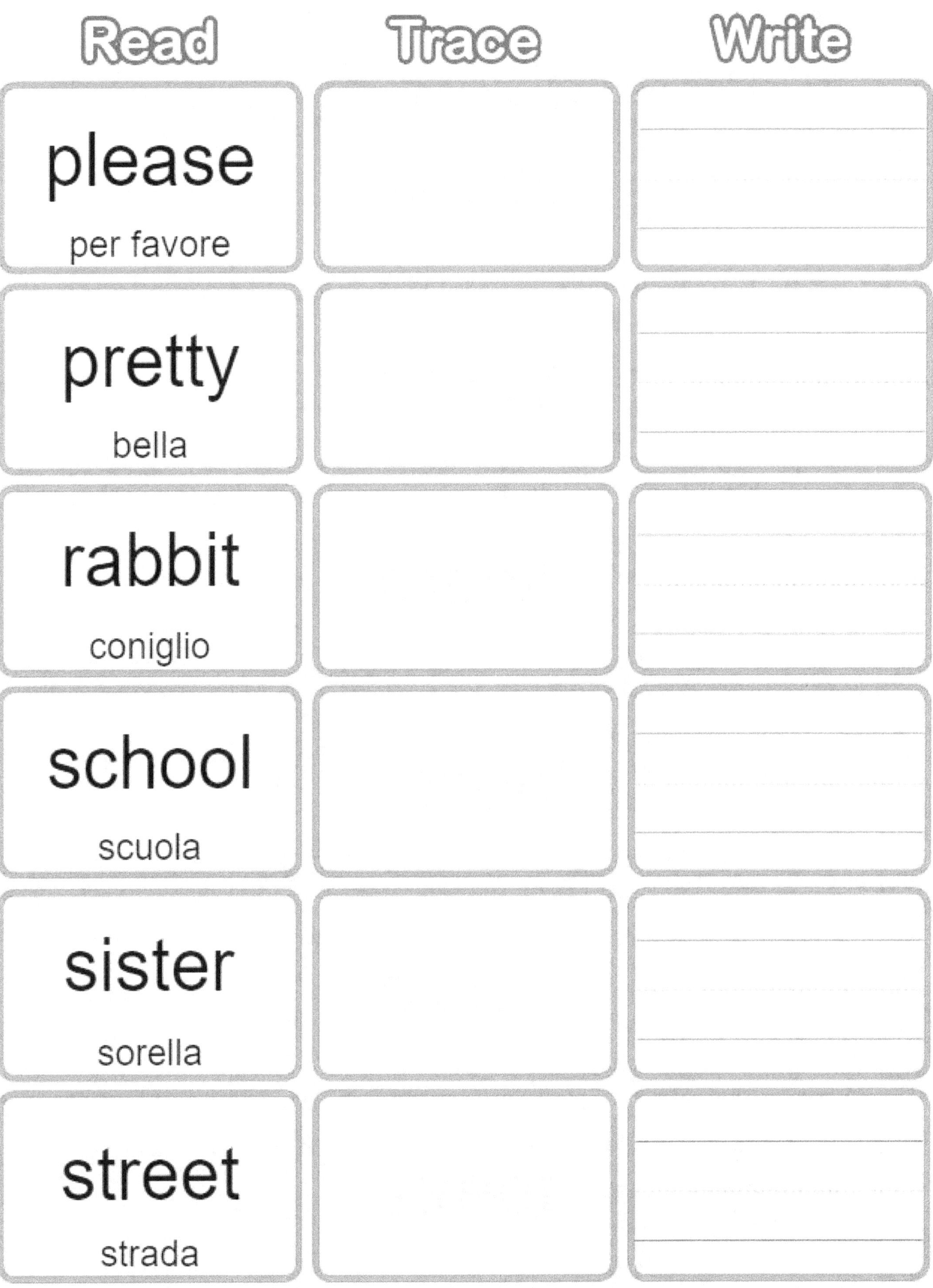

Read	Trace	Write
please per favore		
pretty bella		
rabbit coniglio		
school scuola		
sister sorella		
street strada		

Read and write the sentence!

please	Please stop pulling my hair.
pretty	She made the cake very pretty.
rabbit	The rabbit is white and soft.
school	This is the school.
sister	My sister is wearing a pink dress.
street	They are walking across the street.

Read	Trace	Write
window finestra		
yellow giallo		
because perché		
brother fratello		
chicken pollo		
goodbye addio		

Read and write the sentence!

window	The window is open.
yellow	The ducky is yellow.
because	She will sleep because it is night.
brother	His brother is playing with him.
chicken	The chicken has hatched out of the egg.
goodbye	The animal is saying goodbye.

Read	Trace	Write
morning mattina		
picture immagine		
birthday compleanno		
children bambini		
squirrel scoiattolo		
together insieme		

Read and write the sentence!

morning	He likes to ride his bike in the morning.
picture	He will take a picture.
birthday	Today is my birthday!
children	The children are doing something.
squirrel	The squirrel is cute.
together	They are sharing a bed together.